VICTORY in JESUS

Experiencing
THE POWER
OF CHRIST
in your daily life

Paul Chappell

First published in 2005 by *Striving Together Publications*, a ministry of Lancaster Baptist Church, Lancaster, CA 93535. *Striving Together Publications* is committed to providing tried, trusted, and proven books that will further equip local churches to carry out the Great Commission. Your comments and suggestions are valued.

Striving Together Publications
4020 E. Lancaster Blvd.
Lancaster, CA 93535
800.201.7748

Cover design by Stephen Houk
Layout by Craig Parker
Editing, proofreading, and assistance by Robert Byers, Kayla Nelson, Esther Brown, and Winifred Brunston

ISBN 1-59894-004-X

Printed in the United States of America

Table of Contents

Victory over Fear

Key Verses

"Now upon the first day of the week, very early in the morning, they came unto the sepulchre, bringing the spices which they had prepared, and certain others with them. And they found the stone rolled away from the sepulchre. And they entered in, and found not the body of the Lord Jesus. And it came to pass, as they were much perplexed thereabout, behold, two men stood by them in shining garments: And as they were afraid, and bowed down their faces to the earth, they said unto them, Why seek ye the living among the dead? He is not here, but is risen: remember how he spake unto you when he was yet in Galilee, Saying, The Son of man must be delivered into the hands of sinful men, and be crucified, and the third day rise again. And they remembered his words, And returned from the sepulchre, and told all these things unto the eleven, and to all the rest."—LUKE 24:1–9

Overview

Fear is one of the greatest barriers to living a victorious Christian life. We see people all around us who are gripped by fear and unable to enjoy life. God does not mean for His children to live this way. When we understand and apply the promise of the empty tomb, we experience God's pathway to victory over our fears.

Lesson Theme

God wants us to have victory over the fears that hold so many people in bondage and despair.

Introduction

_____

_____

_____

I. The Fear of _unplanned_ ~~but tame te~~

~~time was ot~~ _circumstances_

A. The Fear of the _women_

"Why seek ye the living among the dead? He is not here, but is risen: remember how he spake unto you when he was yet in Galilee, Saying, The Son of man must be delivered into the hands of sinful men, and be crucified, and the third day rise again. And they remembered his words."—LUKE 24:5–8

"Thy testimonies also are my delight and my counsellors."—PSALM 119:24

B. The Fear of the _disciples_

II. The Fear of _unmet_ _expectations_

A. Peter's _denial_

"And the second time the cock crew. And Peter called to mind the word that Jesus said unto him, Before the cock *crow twice, thou shalt deny me thrice. And when he thought thereon, he wept."*—MARK 14:72

"But go your way, tell his disciples and Peter that he goeth before you into Galilee: there shall ye see him, as he said unto you."—MARK 16:7

B. Thomas' ___Faith~~ doubt~~___

"For God hath not given us the spirit of fear; but of power, and of love, and of a sound mind."—2 TIMOTHY 1:7

III. The Fear of an ___unknown~~the~~___ ___future___

A. Jesus Prophesied _____

   1. HE PROPHESIED HIS _____
       _____

   "Then saith Jesus unto them, All ye shall be offended because of me this night: for it is written, I will smite the shepherd, and the sheep of the flock shall be scattered abroad. But after I am risen again, I will go before you into Galilee."—MATTHEW 26:31–32

   2. HE PROPHESIED HIS _____
       _____

   "Let not your heart be troubled: ye believe in God, believe also in me. In my Father's house are many mansions: if it were not so, I would have told you. I go to prepare a place for you. And if I go and prepare a place for you, I will come again, and receive you unto

myself; that where I am, there ye may be also."
—JOHN 14:1–3

B. Jesus Prophesied _____

_____

"And said unto them, Thus it is written, and thus it behoved Christ to suffer, and to rise from the dead the third day: And that repentance and remission of sins should be preached in his name among all nations, beginning at Jerusalem."—LUKE 24:46–47

1. ALL HAVE _____

"There is none righteous, no, not one. For all have sinned, and come short of the glory of God."
—ROMANS 3:10; 23

2. ALL MAY HAVE _____

_____

"For God so loved the world, that he gave his only begotten Son, that whosoever believeth in him should not perish, but have everlasting life."—JOHN 3:16

Conclusion

"These things I have spoken unto you, that in me ye might have peace. In the world ye shall have tribulation: but be of good cheer; I have overcome the world."—JOHN 16:33

_____

_____

Study Questions

1. What were the first emotions registered at the tomb?

2. What relieved the disciples' fear of unplanned circumstances?

3. What can lead to despondency and cause us to make poor decisions?

4. What happens when we let worry, fear, and despondency dominate our thinking?

5. Who refused to believe the good news that Jesus had risen again?

6.   What truth does the empty tomb illustrate?

7.   What gives us the confidence to face and overcome our fears?

8.   List some fears in your life. How are you going to overcome them?

Memory Verse

"These things I have spoken unto you, that in me ye might have peace. In the world ye shall have tribulation: but be of good cheer; I have overcome the world."—JOHN 16:33

Victory over Temptation

Key Verses

"And Jesus being full of the Holy Ghost returned from Jordan, and was led by the Spirit into the wilderness, Being forty days tempted of the devil. And in those days he did eat nothing: and when they were ended, he afterward hungered. And the devil said unto him, If thou be the Son of God, command this stone that it be made bread. And Jesus answered him, saying, It is written, That man shall not live by bread alone, but by every word of God. And the devil, taking him up into an high mountain, shewed unto him all the kingdoms of the world in a moment of time. And the devil said unto him, All this power will I give thee, and the glory of them: for that is delivered unto me; and to whomsoever I will I give it. If thou therefore wilt worship me, all shall be thine. And Jesus answered and said unto him, Get thee behind me, Satan: for it is written, Thou shalt worship the Lord thy God, and him only shalt thou serve. And he brought him to Jerusalem, and set him on a pinnacle of the temple, and said unto him, If thou be the Son of God, cast thyself down from hence: For it is written, He shall give his angels charge over thee, to keep thee: And in their hands they shall bear thee up, lest at any time thou dash thy foot against a stone. And Jesus answering said unto him, It is said, Thou shalt not tempt the Lord thy God. And when the devil had ended all the temptation, he departed from him for a season."—LUKE 4:1–13

Overview

If we intend to have victory in the Christian life and in the Lord Jesus Christ, there is one thing that is vital for us to know. We have an adversary who is going to fight us every step of the way. Since the beginning of time, Satan has never wanted God's people to know the joy and the victory of a right relationship with Him. He does not want us to experience victory today. It is his desire to push us away from the things of God.

Lesson Theme

Living a victorious life requires learning how to overcome the temptation to do wrong that each of us faces every day.

Introduction

_____

_____

_____

I. The Pattern of _Temptation_

A. *The Temptation of* _flesh_

B. *The Temptation of* _ambition_

C. *The Temptation of* _Pride and_
confatarlin

II. The Power of _Scriptures_

A. *They* _Promise_ *a Way of Escape*
"Thy word have I hid in mine heart, that I might not sin
against thee."—PSALM 119:11

B. *They* _Provide_ *a Way of Escape*

III. The Promise _to the Temptation_

A. *There Is Victory in* _word of God_
"It is written, That man shall not live by bread alone, but
by every word of God."—Luke 4:4

B. There Is Victory in _Shortwirty to God_

C. There Is Victory in _____

Conclusion

"For we have not an high priest which cannot be touched with the feeling of our infirmities; but was in all points tempted like as we are, yet without sin. Let us therefore come boldly unto the throne of grace, that we may obtain mercy, and find grace to help in time of need."—HEBREWS 4:15–16

_____

_____

_____

Study Questions

1. Why did Jesus suffer temptations and trials?

2. Name three things that Satan uses to tempt believers.

3. Why did the devil want to divert and tempt Jesus Christ?

4. What do we often trade for eternal rewards?

5. Why do most people have trouble resisting temptation?

6. What three things give us the victory when we are facing temptation?

7. How do we become mature, victorious Christians?

8. Satan knows our weaknesses. He will often tempt us with things that appeal to our needs or desires. What are some areas of weakness in your life? How are you going to resist Satan in the midst of temptation?

Memory Verse

"There hath no temptation taken you but such as is common to man: but God is faithful, who will not suffer you to be tempted above that ye are able; but will with the temptation also make a way to escape, that ye may be able to bear it."
—1 CORINTHIANS 10:13

Victory over Stress

Key Verses

"Now it came to pass, as they went, that he entered into a certain village: and a certain woman named Martha received him into her house. And she had a sister called Mary, which also sat at Jesus' feet, and heard his word. But Martha was cumbered about much serving, and came to him, and said, Lord, dost thou not care that my sister hath left me to serve alone? bid her therefore that she help me. And Jesus answered and said unto her, Martha, Martha, thou art careful and troubled about many things: But one thing is needful: and Mary hath chosen that good part, which shall not be taken away from her."—LUKE 10:38–42

Overview

Every church and home needs people who are committed and dedicated workers. Martha was not a bad person. Her spirit of serving and caring is worthy of praise. The problem is that the extreme "Martha Syndrome" can take over our lives without us even realizing it to the point that we become a detriment to the spirit of our family, our work, and our church. We can get to the place where we do not have the joy and victory Jesus wants us to enjoy.

Lesson Theme

Freedom from the tyranny of stress and pressure can be ours when we learn God's pattern for living.

Introduction

_____

_____

_____

I. The _____Pall_____ of Mary

A. A _____peaitful_____ Pace

"*Be still, and know that I am God: I will be exalted among the heathen, I will be exalted in the earth.*"
—PSALM 46:10

"*Wait on the LORD: be of good courage, and he shall strengthen thine heart: wait, I say, on the LORD.*"
—PSALM 27:14

B. A _____opding_____ Pace

   1. RENEW YOUR _____focet_____

   2. RENEW YOUR _____faith_____

   3. RENEW YOUR _____fervency_____

"*O God, thou art my God; early will I seek thee: my soul thirsteth for thee, my flesh longeth for thee in a dry and thirsty land, where no water is.*"—PSALM 63:1

"*Not slothful in business; fervent in spirit; serving the Lord.*"—ROMANS 12:11

II. The _place_ of Mary

A. A _humble_ Place

B. An _honorary_ Place

III. The _purpose_ of Mary

A. A _spiritual_ Purpose

"Neither have I gone back from the commandment of his lips; I have esteemed the words of his mouth more than my necessary food."—JOB 23:12

"Open thou mine eyes, that I may behold wondrous things out of thy law."—PSALM 119:18

"And in the morning, rising up a great while before day, he went out, and departed into a solitary place, and there prayed."—MARK 1:35

B. An _active_ Purpose

Conclusion

_____

_____

_____

Study Questions

1. Define the extreme "Martha Syndrome."

2. Who knew the secret of living in peace rather than living under pressure?

3. How can we enjoy victory over stress?

4. Name three ways you can experience spiritual renewal.

5. What is the greatest honor in life?

6. What are some practical steps to help you develop a passion for the Word of God?

7. How can we remove the stress of daily living?

8. Are you experiencing the extreme "Martha Syndrome"? What must you do to claim the victory during stressful situations?

Memory Verse

"But they that wait upon the Lord shall renew their strength; they shall mount up with wings as eagles, they shall run, and not be weary; and they shall walk, and not faint."
—ISAIAH 40:31

Victory over the Culture

Key Verses

"Paul, an apostle of Jesus Christ by the will of God, according to the promise of life which is in Christ Jesus, To Timothy, my dearly beloved son: Grace, mercy, and peace, from God the Father and Christ Jesus our Lord. I thank God, whom I serve from my forefathers with pure conscience, that without ceasing I have remembrance of thee in my prayers night and day; Greatly desiring to see thee, being mindful of thy tears, that I may be filled with joy; When I call to remembrance the unfeigned faith that is in thee, which dwelt first in thy grandmother Lois, and thy mother Eunice; and I am persuaded that in thee also. Wherefore I put thee in remembrance that thou stir up the gift of God, which is in thee by the putting on of my hands. For God hath not given us the spirit of fear; but of power, and of love, and of a sound mind. Be not thou therefore ashamed of the testimony of our Lord, nor of me his prisoner: but be thou partaker of the afflictions of the gospel according to the power of God; Who hath saved us, and called us with an holy calling, not according to our works, but according to his own purpose and grace, which was given us in Christ Jesus before the world began, But is now made manifest by the appearing of our Saviour Jesus Christ, who hath abolished death, and hath brought life and immortality to light through the gospel."
—2 TIMOTHY 1:1–10

Overview

The constant enemy of every Christian is the degradation of our culture. The prevailing thought process of "live and let live" has permeated our society and is even affecting the church. Even though the culture is becoming more and more wicked, we can succeed in following God and rearing our children to do so as well. We can have victory over the culture.

Lesson Theme

We can rise above the negative effects of the culture and live a life of faith that pleases God.

Introduction

_____

_____

_____

I. Victory in a _Real faith_

A. It Was a Faith that _reruske God love_

_____

B. It Was a Faith that _reruske faith_

_____

"For God hath not given us the spirit of fear; but of power, and of love, and of a sound mind."—2 TIMOTHY 1:7

II. Victory in a _loving family_

A. Wives _encorge_ **their Husbands**

B. Husbands _loves_ **their Wives**

"Her children arise up, and call her blessed; her husband also, and he praiseth her."—PROVERBS 31:28

C. Parents Provide _conif_

III. Victory in a _purpose fuaure_

A. God Has a _purpose_ **for His Children**

B. God Has a ___*plan*___ for His Children

   1. GOD SAVES THROUGH THE _____

"But is now made manifest by the appearing of our Saviour Jesus Christ, who hath abolished death, and hath brought life and immortality to light through the gospel."—2 TIMOTHY 1:10

"My sheep hear my voice, and I know them, and they follow me: And I give unto them eternal life; and they shall never perish, neither shall any man pluck them out of my hand."—JOHN 10:27–28

   2. GOD REPLACED _____ WITH
       IMMORTALITY THROUGH THE _____

"I am the resurrection, and the life: he that believeth in me, though he were dead, yet shall he live."
—JOHN 11:25

Conclusion

_____

_____

_____

Study Questions

1. Describe Timothy's background and culture.

2. What are some of the characteristics of genuine faith?

3. Name some elements of a successful Christian home.

4. What gives us the strength to keep going forward in a backward culture?

5. What is the definition of true success?

6. List some of God's purposes for your life.

7. What is a powerful influence in helping us overcome the allure of the world?

8. Satan is using the influence of our culture to destroy Christians. How can you protect yourself and the lives of your family from evil influences?

Memory Verse

"For whatsoever is born of God overcometh the world: and this is the victory that overcometh the world, even our faith. Who is he that overcometh the world, but he that believeth that Jesus is the Son of God?"—1 JOHN 5:4–5

Victory over Adversity

Key Verses

"Beloved, think it not strange concerning the fiery trial which is to try you, as though some strange thing happened unto you: But rejoice, inasmuch as ye are partakers of Christ's sufferings; that, when his glory shall be revealed, ye may be glad also with exceeding joy. If ye be reproached for the name of Christ, happy are ye; for the spirit of glory and of God resteth upon you: on their part he is evil spoken of, but on your part he is glorified. But let none of you suffer as a murderer, or as a thief, or as an evildoer, or as a busybody in other men's matters. Yet if any man suffer as a Christian, let him not be ashamed; but let him glorify God on this behalf."—1 PETER 4:12–16

Overview

If there is a common thread that runs through the human race, aside from our depravity and sinful nature, it is suffering. Every one of us faces difficulty, trials, and adversity. Adversity in our lives is like a rock thrown into a still pond. First, there is the initial impact, but it certainly doesn't end there. The ripples spread out further and further until they reach the shoreline. While adversity has rippling effects, it can be overcome through Jesus Christ.

Lesson Theme

No matter what difficulties and adversities come into our lives, we can triumph over suffering by understanding the purposes of God.

Introduction

_____

_____

I.   The ___commonality___ of Trials

"Beloved, think it not strange concerning the fiery trial which is to try you."—1 PETER 4:12

    A. Adversity Is ___expable___ in the Life of a Christian

    B. Adversity Is a ___Boof___ of Salvation

II. The ___commendation___ to the Christian

    A. There Is Victory in ___identifying___ with Christ

"But rejoice, inasmuch as ye are partakers of Christ's sufferings."—1 PETER 4:13

    B. There Is Victory in the ___presence___ of God

"If ye be reproached for the name of Christ, happy are ye; for the spirit of glory and of God resteth upon you."—1 PETER 4:14

III. The ___caution___ to the Christian

"But let none of you suffer as a murderer, or as a thief, or as an evildoer, or as a busybody in other men's matters."—1 PETER 4:15

A. Avoid Self-Imposed _Suffering_

B. _Honor_ **Christ when Suffering for His Sake**

    1. DON'T BE _____ OF CHRIST

"For the which cause I also suffer these things: nevertheless I am not ashamed: for I know whom I have believed, and am persuaded that he is able to keep that which I have committed unto him against that day."—2 TIMOTHY 1:12

    2. _____ GOD ON BEHALF OF CHRIST

"I have glorified thee on the earth: I have finished the work which thou gavest me to do."—JOHN 17:4

"Ye are the salt of the earth: but if the salt have lost his savour, wherewith shall it be salted? it is thenceforth good for nothing, but to be cast out, and to be trodden under foot of men. Ye are the light of the world. A city that is set on an hill cannot be hid. Neither do men light a candle, and put it under a bushel, but on a candlestick; and it giveth light unto all that are in the house. Let your light so shine before men, that they may see your good works, and glorify your Father which is in heaven."—MATTHEW 5:13–16

Conclusion

Study Questions

1. What is God's way of maturing a believer?

2. What helps us to persevere and be steadfast in the face of trials?

3. What should be our view of suffering?

4. Name some ways we can experience victory over adversity.

5. Faithfulness in adversity gives us a good opportunity to witness. Why?

6. How can we honor Christ through adverse situations?

7. What adversities are you facing in your life today?

8. How will you apply these truths during trials and
    adversities?

Memory Verse

*"And he said unto me, My grace is sufficient for thee: for my
strength is made perfect in weakness. Most gladly therefore
will I rather glory in my infirmities, that the power of Christ
may rest upon me. Therefore I take pleasure in infirmities,
in reproaches, in necessities, in persecutions, in distresses for
Christ's sake: for when I am weak, then am I strong."*
—2 CORINTHIANS 12:9–10

Victory over the World

Memory Verse

"Whosoever believeth that Jesus is the Christ is born of God: and every one that loveth him that begat loveth him also that is begotten of him. By this we know that we love the children of God, when we love God, and keep his commandments. For this is the love of God, that we keep his commandments: and his commandments are not grievous. For whatsoever is born of God overcometh the world: and this is the victory that overcometh the world, even our faith. Who is he that overcometh the world, but he that believeth that Jesus is the Son of God?"—1 JOHN 5:1–5

Overview

Christians are leaving their faith for the love of the world. All of us need to be aware of the battle between following Christ and following the world. It is impossible to do both. Many Christians are trying to straddle the fence by loving God and the world at the same time. That is impossible. James said, *"Know ye not that the friendship of the world is enmity with God?"* (James 4:4).

Lesson Theme

Gaining victory over the world system that operates in opposition to God requires a real and growing faith.

Introduction

_____

_____

_____

"These things I have spoken unto you, that in me ye might have peace. In the world ye shall have tribulation: but be of good cheer; I have overcome the world."—JOHN 16:33

I. Faith in God's _____*purpose*_____

   A. God's Purpose Is _____*according to His*_____
     timetable

"Trust in the Lord with all thine heart; and lean not unto thine own understanding. In all thy ways acknowledge him, and he shall direct thy paths."—PROVERBS 3:5–6

   B. God's Purpose Is _____*analfs Trust natly*_____

II. Faith in God's _____*precepts*_____

"I will meditate in thy precepts, and have respect unto thy ways."—PSALM 119:15

   A. Trusting His Commandments _____*proves*_____
     our love

"I have kept thy precepts and thy testimonies: for all my ways are before thee."—PSALM 119:168

B. Trusting His Commandments _provides_
our strong

"Thy words were found, and I did eat them; and thy word was unto me the joy and rejoicing of mine heart: for I am called by thy name, O LORD God of hosts."—JEREMIAH 15:16

III. Faith in God's _person_

"These things I have spoken unto you, that in me ye might have peace. In the world ye shall have tribulation: but be of good cheer; I have overcome the world."—JOHN 16:33

A. Jesus is the _____ **One**

B. Jesus Is the _____ **One**
"Neither is there salvation in any other: for there is none other name under heaven given among men, whereby we must be saved."—ACTS 4:12

C. Jesus Is the _____ **One**
"All power is given unto me in heaven and in earth."
—MATTHEW 28:18

"Greater is he that is in you, than he that is in the world."
—1 JOHN 4:4

Conclusion

_____

_____

_____

Study Questions

1. How would you define world in the context of 1 John 5:4?

2. What is God's plan and design for us?

3. State the opposite of faith.

4. What is the relationship between the Scriptures and faith?

5. What gives us strength to overcome the world?

6. Explain the significance of the name Christ.

7. Who is the source of victory?

8. When was the last time you dealt with spiritual opposition? How did you handle this trial?

Memory Verse

"*These things I have spoken unto you, that in me ye might have peace. In the world ye shall have tribulation: but be of good cheer; I have overcome the world.*"—JOHN 16:33

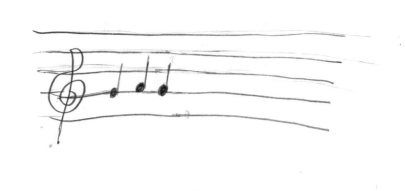

Victory over Scoffers

Key Verses

"This second epistle, beloved, I now write unto you; in both which I stir up your pure minds by way of remembrance: That ye may be mindful of the words which were spoken before by the holy prophets, and of the commandment of us the apostles of the Lord and Saviour: Knowing this first, that there shall come in the last days scoffers, walking after their own lusts, And saying, Where is the promise of his coming? for since the fathers fell asleep, all things continue as they were from the beginning of the creation. For this they willingly are ignorant of, that by the word of God the heavens were of old, and the earth standing out of the water and in the water: Whereby the world that then was, being overflowed with water, perished: But the heavens and the earth, which are now, by the same word are kept in store, reserved unto fire against the day of judgment and perdition of ungodly men. But, beloved, be not ignorant of this one thing, that one day is with the Lord as a thousand years, and a thousand years as one day. The Lord is not slack concerning his promise, as some men count slackness; but is longsuffering to us-ward, not willing that any should perish, but that all should come to repentance. But the day of the Lord will come as a thief in the night; in the which the heavens shall pass away with a great noise, and the elements shall melt with fervent heat, the earth also and the works that are therein shall be burned up."—2 PETER 3:1–10

Overview

In America today we see scoffers attacking the underlying principles of our Christian faith. Scoffers intentionally endeavor to turn truth into ridicule. Their purpose is to depreciate the value of truth in the eyes of society. They come in mockery. Their spirit and temperament indicate no desire to find the truth. They take up the Bible with the design of finding things to ridicule and discredit. God's Word tells us how we can overcome these critics.

Lesson Theme

As our faith grows, our confidence in God and His Word can overcome anything that scoffers and critics say against us.

Introduction

_____

_____

_____

I. Victory through God's *promise*

A. The Words of the *prophets*

"*Of which salvation the prophets have inquired and searched diligently, who prophesied of the grace that should come unto you: Searching what, or what manner of time the Spirit of Christ which was in them did signify, when it testified beforehand the sufferings of Christ, and the glory that should follow.*"—1 PETER 1:10–11

B. The Words of the *apostles*

C. The Words of the *Lord*

II. Victory through God's *power*

A. The Power to *create*

"*Through faith we understand that the worlds were framed by the word of God, so that things which are seen were not made of things which do appear.*"—HEBREWS 11:3

"*For he spake, and it was done.*"—PSALM 33:9

B. The Power to _destroy_

C. The Power to _judg_
"And as it is appointed unto men once to die, but after this the judgment."—HEBREWS 9:27

III. Victory through God's _rationate_

A. The Promise of His _____

    1. ACCORDING TO HIS _____
    "For a thousand years in thy sight are but as yesterday when it is past, and as a watch in the night."—PSALM 90:4

    2. ACCORDING TO HIS _____

B. The Promise of _____

Conclusion

_____

_____

_____

Study Questions

1. How can we obtain victory over scoffers?

2. What should be our response to those critics who question the validity of the Bible?

3. Who gave testimony to the reliability of Scripture?

4. What opens our understanding of the Bible?

5. Many times we as believers support the scoffer's case. How?

6. What does Noah's ark symbolize?

7. What promises from God's Word oppose unbelieving critics?

8. How have you dealt with those who are critical of your faith?

Memory Verse

"Woe unto them that call evil good, and good evil; that put darkness for light, and light for darkness; that put bitter for sweet, and sweet for bitter!"—ISAIAH 5:20

Victory over Family Turmoil

Key Verses

"*And he said, A certain man had two sons: And the younger of them said to his father, Father, give me the portion of goods that falleth to me. And he divided unto them his living. And not many days after the younger son gathered all together, and took his journey into a far country, and there wasted his substance with riotous living. And when he had spent all, there arose a mighty famine in that land; and he began to be in want. And he went and joined himself to a citizen of that country; and he sent him into his fields to feed swine. And he would fain have filled his belly with the husks that the swine did eat: and no man gave unto him. And when he came to himself, he said, How many hired servants of my father's have bread enough and to spare, and I perish with hunger! I will arise and go to my father, and will say unto him, Father, I have sinned against heaven, and before thee, And am no more worthy to be called thy son: make me as one of thy hired servants. And he arose, and came to his father. But when he was yet a great way off, his father saw him, and had compassion, and ran, and fell on his neck, and kissed him. And the son said unto him, Father, I have sinned against heaven, and in thy sight, and am no more worthy to be called thy son. But the father said to his servants, Bring forth the best robe, and put it on him; and put a ring on his hand, and shoes on his feet: And bring hither the fatted calf, and kill it; and let us eat, and be merry: For this my son was dead, and is alive again; he was lost, and is found. And they began to be merry.*"—LUKE 15:11–24

Overview

Every family faces problems from time to time. While God intended the family to be a place of joy and security, the entrance of sin into the world introduced turmoil. Many families have been completely derailed from following God by turmoil. Other families are strengthened and find victory over the turmoil. The difference in the outcome is determined by how they respond when the turmoil comes.

Lesson Theme

Following God's plan for restoring relationships can bring peace to any family, no matter what sort of turmoil may come into their lives.

Introduction

_____

_____

_____

I. The _Reason_ for Family Turmoil

A. *Focus on* _Self_

B. *Rejection of* _Structure_

C. *Decision to* _Sin_

II. The _Remedy_ for Family Unity

"For we must needs die, and are as water spilt on the ground, which cannot be gathered up again; neither doth God respect any person: yet doth he devise means, that his banished be not expelled from him."—2 SAMUEL 14:14

A. ____Realization____ *of Sin*

B. ____Repentance____ *of Sin*

"I will arise and go to my father, and will say unto him, Father, I have sinned against heaven, and before thee."
—LUKE 15:18

"Against thee, thee only, have I sinned, and done this evil in thy sight: that thou mightest be justified when thou speakest, and be clear when thou judgest."—PSALM 51:4

III. The _Restration_ of Family Joy

    A. _forgiveive_

    B. _____

"Let him turn to his own house, and let him not see my face."—2 SAMUEL 14:24

Conclusion

_____

_____

_____

Study Questions

1. What is the root cause of most family turmoil?

2. God compares rebellion to what sin?

3. What are we implying when we reject God's structure and rules?

4. Before restoration can heal conflict, what must occur?

5. Define true repentance.

6. Name two components to the restoration of family joy.

7. When did seeds of rebellion grow in Absalom's heart?

8. Your family may be affected by trouble and turmoil today. How can you seek to restore joy and fellowship in your home?

Memory Verse

"Except the Lord build the house, they labour in vain that build it: except the Lord keep the city, the watchman waketh but in vain."—PSALM 127:1

Victory over Injustice

Key Verses

"I beseech thee for my son Onesimus, whom I have begotten in my bonds: Which in time past was to thee unprofitable, but now profitable to thee and to me: Whom I have sent again: thou therefore receive him, that is, mine own bowels: Whom I would have retained with me, that in thy stead he might have ministered unto me in the bonds of the gospel: But without thy mind would I do nothing; that thy benefit should not be as it were of necessity, but willingly. For perhaps he therefore departed for a season, that thou shouldest receive him for ever; Not now as a servant, but above a servant, a brother beloved, specially to me, but how much more unto thee, both in the flesh, and in the Lord? If thou count me therefore a partner, receive him as myself. If he hath wronged thee, or oweth thee ought, put that on mine account; I Paul have written it with mine own hand, I will repay it: albeit I do not say to thee how thou owest unto me even thine own self besides."—PHILEMON 10–19

Overview

We are going to experience unfair circumstances in our lives. Injustice is written throughout history. It is not only cultural and historical, but is frequently very personal. Situations come into all of our lives that are simply unfair. The question is not whether we will face injustice, but rather how will we respond when we do face it. By following the pattern outlined in God's Word, we can overcome injustice.

Lesson Theme

Properly responding to injustice allows us to take advantage of opportunities God brings into our lives to reach others with the Gospel.

Introduction

_____

_____

_____

I. The _reality_ of Injustice

A. Onesimus Was _cost_ an Unprofitable Servant

"Therefore if any man be in Christ, he is a new creature: old things are passed away; behold, all things are become new."—2 CORINTHIANS 5:17

B. Onesimus Was _Saved_, but Still Suffering

II. The _Revelation_ of Christian Grace

A. _Love_ Every Believer in Christ

B. _Excuse_ Every Believer in Christ

"At my first answer no man stood with me, but all men forsook me: I pray God that it may not be laid to their charge."—2 TIMOTHY 4:16

1. _Receive_ HIM—HE IS PROFITABLE

2. _Relieve_ HIM AS A BROTHER

III. The _Restoration_ of Fellowship

A. Based on _Forgives_

"If thou count me therefore a partner, receive him as myself. If he hath wronged thee, or oweth thee ought, put that on mine account."—Philemon 17–18

B. Brought Great _Joy_

Conclusion

_____

_____

_____

Study Questions

1. What was the name of Philemon's slave?

2. Is injustice a universal dilemma? Name a cultural or historical instance of injustice.

3. During times of persecution or injustice, what should be the focus of mature believers?

4. How can we show God's grace to those who are suffering?

5. What is our job as the children of God?

6. Define reconciliation.

7. Is there someone who has treated you unjustly? Do you harbor hatred or bitterness toward them?

8. What must you do to restore fellowship with those who have treated you unjustly?

Memory Verse

"For this is thankworthy, if a man for conscience toward God endure grief, suffering wrongfully."—1 PETER 2:19

Victory over a Temporal World

Key Verses

"Behold, I shew you a mystery; We shall not all sleep, but we shall all be changed, In a moment, in the twinkling of an eye, at the last trump: for the trumpet shall sound, and the dead shall be raised incorruptible, and we shall be changed. For this corruptible must put on incorruption, and this mortal must put on immortality. So when this corruptible shall have put on incorruption, and this mortal shall have put on immortality, then shall be brought to pass the saying that is written, Death is swallowed up in victory. O death, where is thy sting? O grave, where is thy victory? The sting of death is sin; and the strength of sin is the law. But thanks be to God, which giveth us the victory through our Lord Jesus Christ. Therefore, my beloved brethren, be ye stedfast, unmoveable, always abounding in the work of the Lord, forasmuch as ye know that your labour is not in vain in the Lord."

—1 CORINTHIANS 15:51–58

Overview

We live as if our lives will last forever. We live with ourselves rather than eternity in mind. The poet said, "Only one life, 'twill soon be past; Only what's done for Christ will last." Because of the death of Jesus on the cross and His resurrection, we have victory over the sting of death. We do not need to fear it any longer, for the most that death can do is to usher us into His presence for eternity. The truth of the resurrection and the promise of eternal life give us the opportunity to gain victory over this temporal world in which we live.

Lesson Theme

Properly assessing the brevity of life helps us live in such a way that we bring honor and glory to God.

Introduction

_____

_____

_____

"Wherefore, as by one man sin entered into the world, and death by sin; and so death passed upon all men, for that all have sinned."—ROMANS 5:12

I. The *Reminder* of Life's Brevity

"So teach us to number our days, that we may apply our hearts unto wisdom."—PSALM 90:12

A. God May Call us Home by *death*

"For this God is our God for ever and ever: he will be our guide even unto death."—PSALM 48:14

"Precious in the sight of the LORD is the death of his saints."—PSALM 116:15

"Therefore we are always confident, knowing that, whilst we are at home in the body, we are absent from the Lord: We are confident, I say, and willing rather to be absent from the body, and to be present with the Lord."—2 CORINTHIANS 5:6, 8

B. God May Call us Home by the *Rapture*

II. The _Reassurance_ of Victory

"O sing unto the LORD a new song; for he hath done marvellous things: his right hand, and his holy arm, hath gotten him the victory."—PSALM 98:1

A. Victory Is a _Gift_

"For sin shall not have dominion over you: for ye are not under the law, but under grace."—ROMANS 6:14

B. Victory _comy_ Through Jesus Christ

"There is none other name under heaven given among men, whereby we must be saved."—ACTS 4:12

III. The _Respose_ of a Sincere Christian

"For we are his workmanship, created in Christ Jesus unto good works, which God hath before ordained that we should walk in them."—EPHESIANS 2:10

A. Our Motivation Is _fastion_

B. The Manifestation Is _measnelle_

Conclusion

_____

_____

_____

Study Questions

1. Why is there death in the world?

2. Name the two ways a Christian's life will end.

3. What is the meaning of the word "rapture"?

4. Can we gain victory over a temporal world through our own works?

5. How did Jesus win His victory?

6. What are the responses of a sincere Christian?

7. As a Christian, what should be our focus if we are to gain victory over a temporal world?

8. How are you going to rise above the challenges that stop others from serving the Lord and experiencing the victory through Him?

Memory Verse

"And if I go and prepare a place for you, I will come again, and receive you unto myself; that where I am, there ye may be also."—JOHN 14:3

Victory over the Power of Sin

Key Verses

"What shall we say then? Shall we continue in sin, that grace may abound? God forbid. How shall we, that are dead to sin, live any longer therein? Know ye not, that so many of us as were baptized into Jesus Christ were baptized into his death? Therefore we are buried with him by baptism into death: that like as Christ was raised up from the dead by the glory of the Father, even so we also should walk in newness of life. For if we have been planted together in the likeness of his death, we shall be also in the likeness of his resurrection: Knowing this, that our old man is crucified with him, that the body of sin might be destroyed, that henceforth we should not serve sin. For he that is dead is freed from sin. Now if we be dead with Christ, we believe that we shall also live with him: Knowing that Christ being raised from the dead dieth no more; death hath no more dominion over him. For in that he died, he died unto sin once: but in that he liveth, he liveth unto God. Likewise reckon ye also yourselves to be dead indeed unto sin, but alive unto God through Jesus Christ our Lord. Let not sin therefore reign in your mortal body, that ye should obey it in the lusts thereof. Neither yield ye your members as instruments of unrighteousness unto sin: but yield yourselves unto God, as those that are alive from the dead, and your members as instruments of righteousness unto God."—ROMANS 6:1–13

Overview

Far better than forgiveness of sin is following God's plan to do right in the first place. How much pain and heartbreak would be avoided if we overcame the temptation rather than yielding to it. The church in our day needs a renewed focus on the process of sanctification and the power over sin that Jesus makes available to us. When someone accepts Christ as Saviour, they are immediately justified. Another ongoing process also begins at salvation, and that is sanctification. Understanding the process of sanctification is vital to overcoming the power of sin.

Lesson Theme

A believer who accesses the power of God and yields to Him rather than to sin will gain victory over temptation to do wrong.

Introduction

_____

_____

_____

"If we confess our sins, he is faithful and just to forgive us our sins, and to cleanse us from all unrighteousness."—1 JOHN 1:9

I. ____Refuse____ to Presume upon the ____Grace____ of God

A. Grace Is not a ____License____ to Sin
"For, brethren, ye have been called unto liberty; only use not liberty for an occasion to the flesh, but by love serve one another."—GALATIANS 5:13

B. Grace Is a ____motivation____ to Serve
"As free, and not using your liberty for a cloke of maliciousness, but as the servants of God."—1 PETER 2:16

"Let no corrupt communication proceed out of your mouth, but that which is good to the use of edifying, that it may minister grace unto the hearers."—EPHESIANS 4:29

II. ____Remember____ the ____Picture____ of Baptism

A. We Identified with His ____Death____

67

"Knowing this, that our old man is crucified with him, that the body of sin might be destroyed, that henceforth we should not serve sin."—Romans 6:6

B. We Identified with His _Resurreccion_
"Therefore if any man be in Christ, he is a new creature: old things are passed away; behold, all things are become new."—2 CORINTHIANS 5:17

"O death, where is thy sting? O grave, where is thy victory? The sting of death is sin; and the strength of sin is the law."—1 CORINTHIANS 15:55–56

III. _Reckon_ Ourselves Alive to God

"Likewise reckon ye also yourselves to be dead indeed unto sin, but alive unto God through Jesus Christ our Lord."
—Romans 6:11

A. We Are _dead_ **to** _Sin_ **Because of the Cross**

B. We Are _____ **to** _____ **through Christ**

Conclusion

_____

_____

_____

Study Questions
1. What is far better than the forgiveness of sins?

2. Is grace a license to sin?

3. What is the product of grace in the heart and life of a Christian?

4. Define grace.

5. What does baptism represent?

6. When was the old nature defeated?

7. What happens if we do not apply the truth of the cross?

8. You have accepted Jesus Christ as your Saviour. Are you living in the newness of His life? Are you enjoying victory over the power of sin?

Memory Verse

"For he hath made him to be sin for us, who knew no sin; that we might be made the righteousness of God in him."
—2 CORINTHIANS 5:21

Victory over National Decline

Key Verses

"And the LORD appeared to Solomon by night, and said unto him, I have heard thy prayer, and have chosen this place to myself for an house of sacrifice. If I shut up heaven that there be no rain, or if I command the locusts to devour the land, or if I send pestilence among my people; If my people, which are called by my name, shall humble themselves, and pray, and seek my face, and turn from their wicked ways; then will I hear from heaven, and will forgive their sin, and will heal their land. Now mine eyes shall be open, and mine ears attent unto the prayer that is made in this place."—2 CHRONICLES 7:12–15

Overview

Although our nation has a great heritage, we would also have to admit that the spiritual, moral, and family situation in our country today is desperately in need of revival and a return to the faith of our fathers. God gives us a prescription for national revival and renewal. Sometimes as we look around at our nation that has turned away from God, we wonder "What can we do?" "Where can we begin?" When we need help from Heaven, we must begin with an honest evaluation of our own lives. As individual Christians, we can make a difference for our nation.

Lesson Theme

The decline of morals and character we are seeing in America today will only be reversed by following God's plan for national renewal.

Introduction

_____

_____

_____

I. Seek Personal _Reinel_

A. My _People_

B. My _name_

II. Seek Prayerful _Renewal_

A. _Humble_ **Themselves**

"The LORD is nigh unto them that are of a broken heart;
and saveth such as be of a contrite spirit."—PSALM 34:18

B. _Prayer_

III. Seek Powerful _Restortion_

"If my people, which are called by my name, shall humble
themselves, and pray, and seek my face, and turn from their
wicked ways; then will I hear from heaven, and will forgive
their sin, and will heal their land."—2 CHRONICLES 7:14

A. God Will _Hear_

"Hear me, O LORD, hear me, that this people may know that thou art the LORD God, and that thou hast turned their heart back again."—1 KINGS 18:37

B. God Will _Forgive_

"For thou, Lord, art good, and ready to forgive; and plenteous in mercy unto all them that call upon thee."
—PSALM 86:5

"In whom we have redemption through his blood, the forgiveness of sins, according to the riches of his grace."
—EPHESIANS 1:7

C. God Will _Heal_

"Wilt thou not revive us again: that thy people may rejoice in thee?"—PSALM 85:6

Conclusion

_____

_____

_____

Study Questions

1. What brings an awareness of God?

2. Are we all God's children? Explain your answer.

3. What are the prerequisites for prayerful renewal?

4. Why is God's promise of revival conditional?

5. What is God's promise to us in Psalm 86:5?

6. What must happen before people will sacrifice for the common good of their country?

7. What is the answer to our national problems?

8. If national revival will not come until we ask God to revive us individually, what must you do to experience restoration and renewal?

Memory Verse
"Wilt thou not revive us again: that thy people may rejoice in thee?"—PSALM 85:6

Victory over a Wounded Spirit

Key Verses

*"Wherefore seeing we also are compassed about with so great
a cloud of witnesses, let us lay aside every weight, and the sin
which doth so easily beset us, and let us run with patience
the race that is set before us, Looking unto Jesus the author
and finisher of our faith; who for the joy that was set before
him endured the cross, despising the shame, and is set down
at the right hand of the throne of God. For consider him that
endured such contradiction of sinners against himself, lest ye
be wearied and faint in your minds. Ye have not yet resisted
unto blood, striving against sin. And ye have forgotten the
exhortation which speaketh unto you as unto children, My
son, despise not thou the chastening of the Lord, nor faint
when thou art rebuked of him: For whom the Lord loveth he
chasteneth, and scourgeth every son whom he receiveth. If
ye endure chastening, God dealeth with you as with sons; for
what son is he whom the father chasteneth not? But if ye be
without chastisement, whereof all are partakers, then are ye
bastards, and not sons. Furthermore we have had fathers of
our flesh which corrected us, and we gave them reverence:
shall we not much rather be in subjection unto the Father
of spirits, and live? For they verily for a few days chastened
us after their own pleasure; but he for our profit, that we
might be partakers of his holiness. Now no chastening for
the present seemeth to be joyous, but grievous: nevertheless
afterward it yieldeth the peaceable fruit of righteousness
unto them which are exercised thereby. Wherefore lift up the
hands which hang down, and the feeble knees; And make*

straight paths for your feet, lest that which is lame be turned out of the way; but let it rather be healed. Follow peace with all men, and holiness, without which no man shall see the Lord: Looking diligently lest any man fail of the grace of God; lest any root of bitterness springing up trouble you, and thereby many be defiled; Lest there be any fornicator, or profane person, as Esau, who for one morsel of meat sold his birthright."—HEBREWS 12:1–16

Overview

Many believers today bear the marks of wounded spirits and injuries that they've suffered at some point during their lives. The good news is that even if we have faltered or fallen and been injured, we can still recover and run a good race. Sometimes when defeat and discouragement come, it can wound our spirits. Yet, even if that has happened to us, we can overcome. The Bible tells us how we can triumph over a wounded spirit.

Lesson Theme

Injuries are certain in a sinful world, but we do not have to allow hurts of the past to keep us from reaching God's very best for our lives.

Introduction

_____

_____

_____

I. _____*Look*_____ **to the Saviour**

   A. He Is the ____*originating*____ **One**
"*But thou, Bethlehem Ephratah, though thou be little among the thousands of Judah, yet out of thee shall he come forth unto me that is to be ruler in Israel; whose goings forth have been from of old, from everlasting.*"
—MICAH 5:2

   B. He Is the ____*Enduring*____ **One**

   C. He Is the ____*Resurrected*____ **One**

II. _____*Listen*_____ **to the Saviour**

   A. _____*Listen*_____ **to His Chastening**

   B. _____*Learn*_____ **from His Chastening**

III. _____*Learn*_____ **of the Saviour**

"Take my yoke upon you, and learn of me; for I am meek and lowly in heart: and ye shall find rest unto your souls."
—MATTHEW 11:29

A. Follow His ____Peace____
"Peace I leave with you, my peace I give unto you: not as the world giveth, give I unto you. Let not your heart be troubled, neither let it be afraid."—JOHN 14:27

B. Follow His ____Holies____
"And one cried unto another, and said, Holy, holy, holy, is the LORD of hosts: the whole earth is full of his glory."
—ISAIAH 6:3

C. Forsake all ____Btters____

Conclusion

_____
_____
_____

Study Questions

1. Who should we focus on when our spirit has been injured or wounded?

2. What are some similarities between the Christian life and a race?

3. Jesus sat down when he reached Heaven. Why is this symbolic?

4. What is evidence that we are God's children?

5. What is the purpose of God's chastening?

6. What are some characteristics of Christ that teach us how to endure injury or difficulty?

7. What is the defining characteristic of God?

8. How will you gain the victory when your spirit has been wounded?

Memory Verse

"The spirit of a man will sustain his infirmity; but a wounded spirit who can bear?"—PROVERBS 18:14

For additional Christian
growth resources visit
www.strivingtogether.com